Perigee Moon

Margaret Chula

Perigee Moon is set in Avenir, a geometric typeface by Adrian Frutiger,1987.

ISBN 978-1-952204-07-4
Printed in the United States of America

RED MOUNTAIN PRESS

Seattle, Washington
www.redmountainpress.us

To all women tanka poets writing
from the Heian era to the present day

Also by Margaret Chula

Contents

Introduction: An Urge to Sing

> "The poem is an attitude, and a prayer; it sings on
> the page and it sings itself off the page."
> —*Mary Oliver*

Imagine yourself in the Japanese court seven hundred and fifty years ago. Amid the emperor and empress and all their retainers and special ministers, all dressed in their finest court robes, a *kouji* (poem singer) is chanting a formal sort of poetry called *waka*. Both within and outside the court, these poems praise nature and the seasons, or could be love poems. They sometimes hint at deeper meanings through implied metaphorical references. Then and today, for example, a skylark might represent a lover, and if it's flying over the hills, never to be seen again, the poet's love might remain forever unrequited. Or if the moon's reflection is depicted as rippling on pond water, it could be that the poet's heart is aflutter with passion and desire. In later years, even warriors of the samurai class could not be respected leaders unless they were able to compose these poems on the spot.

This is how tanka poetry evolved in Japan, over thirteen hundred years. As the country of eight islands developed its own written language, expanding on and sometimes departing from the Chinese written script they first adopted, their poetry grew from *uta* (song) to *waka* (Japanese song), and eventually to the genre of tanka (short song) we know today.

In English, tanka is usually five lines in length, often blending descriptions of natural scenes with revelations of the poet's feelings. As with haiku, its much younger cousin, in English a set syllable count need not be followed. Sometimes a pivot occurs in the poem, where one line might be read differently with what precedes it, compared with what follows. As with references to famous places or other allusions, the pivot was a means of compression in the poem, in addition to the compression afforded by possible allegorical interpretation. An extension of Japanese culture itself, tanka was often indirect, merely hinting at meaning, relying on what was not said as much as what was. This is still true today. A turn in the poem gave it an added dimension, creating space in readers' minds and hearts to enable them to enter the poem—to see what the poet saw, to feel what the poet felt.

For those who might be new to tanka, Margaret Chula's *Perigee Moon* may serve as a model for how this poetry is done. And for those who have known tanka for decades and know Chula's vaunted place in its North American unfolding, this book will provide many rewards. Each poem and sequence exhibits her wealth of poetic experience and cultural understanding. She lived in Kyōto for a dozen years and has continued, in Portland, Oregon, to live a life infused with Japanese aesthetics. Tanka does not require this sort of background, but Chula makes the most of hers, giving us poems that represent the flowering of tanka poetry in English. Her gift in these songs is a taste of life where she has lived and traveled, including a taste of Japan and its deep influence on her and her poetry. These are poems by turns energetic and tranquil, written in reverence and yet detachment, pointing to the old as well as the new.

Chula deftly groups her tanka in sections, such as the opening exploration of love poems, in a nod to tanka's primary historical mode. Some of these poems hint at eroticism, and tell of Japanese contexts, such as the Tanabata festival. They are by no means tethered to Japan in any kind of imitative way but share the modern grit and attraction of a Goth girl's underwear or Billie Holiday's crooning. Later sections explore memories of childhood and family, birds and nature, and travels both outer and inner. With the poems in *Perigee Moon* and beyond, Margaret Chula is forever dancing with Japan, her shadow lover.

May you emerge from each reading of this book with the urge to join the singing.

Michael Dylan Welch
Founder and President, Tanka Society of America

ALL THOSE WORDS FOR LOVE

unlike Pygmalion's
marble Galatea
my lover's lips
are pliant and warm
and taste of strawberries

how can I write
a decent tanka
about loneliness
with you beside me
nibbling my neck

folding his clothes
at the laundromat
the backpacker
checks out the Goth girl
and then her underwear

at Trader Vic's
taking the umbrella off
my tequila sunrise
once again I tell you
I'm not that kind of girl

kaleidoscope night
my diaphanous dress
and stiletto heels—
you on an acid trip
with a one-way ticket

now I'm relieved
that you never showed up
for our rendezvous
I was a silly woman
aching for romance

spring peepers
and their sad cheeping
keep me awake
all those sweet nothings
I once thought were something

like a blotter
absorbing the shadows
of your complaints
I hate you for bringing
an end to imagination

garden twilight
a single sparrow twitters
then moves on
you and I, star-crossed
like Tanabata lovers

those half-dead rosebushes
from Thriftway
like you
all they needed was space
to spread their roots

Tanabata: known as the "Star Festival", it commemo-
rates the romance of two lovers, the stars Vega and
Altair, who are united once a year on the seventh day
of the seventh month.

the tireless squirrel
finally tips over the suet
peppered with chili—
those forbidden things that left
a bitter taste in my mouth

how can I fault
the curious Pandora
for opening the jar
I thought my face cream, too
promised eternal youth

after the divorce
Lady Chatterley's Lover
hidden in her drawer—
both Mother and I enthralled
by unrequited love

remembering him—
from deep inside
the stone wall
the faint cries
of crickets

depressing things:
a letter unanswered
buzz of gossip
hawthorn bushes hiding
a hoard of mosquitoes

sudden illness
my husband surprises me
with spring wildflowers
plunked into a jar—
helter-skelter love

just a few blooms
of white trillium
on the Wildwood Trail
how to hold back the blossoms
until you arrive

squawk of a mallard
her mate flies across the pond
to comfort her—
until this moment
I didn't miss you at all

perigee moon—
I dance barefoot
on the new-mown grass
in perfect step
with my shadow lover

birthday cards
tucked into my thesaurus
over the years—
today, they tumble out
all those words for love

"stormy weather"
Billie Holiday croons—
we sit by the fire
and raise a toast to
forty-five years together

SNAPSHOTS

that photo of us
summiting Kala Patthar
at seventeen thousand feet
we were fearless and hungry
for adventure

Balinese festival
your long legs beneath
an ikat sarong
and afterwards our own dance
as geckos chirped from the eaves

thirty years later
we pose at the same temple
November in Kyōto
and the gingko leaves
are still glowing

anniversary
at the Heathman Hotel
in the morning
you shower me
with pink rose petals

SPOTS OF RUST

star gazing
there's Jupiter trying
to outshine the moon
like me, still wanting to impress
my senile mother

in her mid-nineties
Mother shuffles her walker
across the lawn
there must be something
I need at this tag sale

TAKING A TURN

sudden stroke
her life takes a turn
still hanging on
the bathroom peg
Mother's pastel nightgown

those shards of soap
she tucked in her dresser
have stained her sweaters
I box them up and send them
to the Survival Center

moving Mother
into assisted living
on April Fool's Day
we say goodbye
to her battered golf clubs

her personal dresser
I pair blouses and slacks
to bring to Mother
both of us loathing
the pale hospital gowns

only one closet
in the nursing home
Mother hangs
three blouses
on each hanger

childhood Halloweens
I wore a princess costume—
after Mother's stroke
I carve my pumpkin
with a crooked smile

breathing deeply
to prolong
this last visit—
the harvest moon
fades into morning

one daffodil
fallen face down
into a water bowl
Mother's slender neck
as she drank from the stream

red rover, red rover
she was always the last one
to be called over—
my faint-hearted mother
who outlived all her friends

a late bloomer
with two failed marriages
she waited so long
for the Prince of Darkness
to take her away

deadheading
Mother's rhododendrons
that bloomed without me
guilt and remorse
sticky on my hands

after the rain
a few spots of rust
on the new moss
my love was not enough
to keep you in this world

Mother's death day
look how hopefully
chickadees flit
to the empty feeder
again, again, and again

OBON AT THE PORTLAND JAPANESE GARDEN

preparing to light
a commemorative candle
for my mother—
the unexpected giggle
when the wick comes out

after a silent prayer
I launch my candle
on the Upper Pond
hers is the brightest light
floating on the water

lifting tendrils
of the weeping willow
to keep her in sight
Mother's fingers
combing through my hair

the old Buddhist priest
chants the Heart Sutra
one by one
the candles go out
as the moon rises

walking on the path
through the silent garden
we pass stone lanterns
still holding the light
of those we've loved

Obon: a Japanese Buddhist festival to honor the
spirits of one's ancestors

here it comes
her hundredth birthday
without her—
this year's white roses
bloom in profusion

in my dream
Mother is still alive
I fall back to sleep
to finish our stroll
in the summer garden

KEEPSAKES

sixty years gone by
and even now that outrage—
first day of school
and being scolded for playing
with trucks on the boys' side

second grade
the new girl's skin darker
than the others—
her stick-figures drawn
with black Magic Marker

when I was eight
I designed glam outfits
for my paper dolls—
those one-dimensional girls
with the same benign smiles

the bearded lady
how she terrified me
under the big top
and now, in my garden
the yellow iris

discovering
my high school diary
with the small key lock
my life preserved in shorthand
I can no longer read

all those words
said in anger
too late now—
red nubs of rhubarb
poke up through the mud

like a fragile strip
of birch bark
I tear off
the dark scab
of my fear

hard to accept
that our thirty-year friendship
is really over—
waft of a clove cigarette
and my eyes fill with tears

high school reunion
everyone in the room
the same age—
alone on the patio
I count the stars

in the cupboard
of his wet bar
the smell of stale gin
my brother's aftershave
the same as our father's

when I was young
I counted Mother's sighs
disappointments
like those imperfect sand dollars
that she tossed back to sea

                    pumping my legs
                    on the outdoor swing
                    I thought I could fly—
                    today the air is full
                    of yellow butterflies

autumn rain
darkens the sidewalk
I, too, was that girl
with flaxen hair
and red rubber boots

never daring
carve my initials
into tree bark
my childhood birch pockmarked
with woodpecker holes

tomato starts
first the yellow blossoms
then the red fruit—
be careful, my sweet
of who you let pluck you

early summer
buttercups by the roadside
are already dusty
at age twenty, she tells me
she's weary of the world

awakening
to robin song
those spring mornings
when Mother and I sipped tea
from porcelain cups

cradled in my palm
my baby sister's ashes
and shards of bones—
remembering how I envied
her high cheekbones

her laughter too bright
as she squints at the sun
in her backpack
a half-empty fifth
of cheap vodka

reading the poems
of my departed friend
her melancholy life
like a white gardenia
worn in dirty hair

SOUND OF PEEPERS

taking flight
a brown pelican
flaps its heavy wings
click of a playing card
on my bicycle spokes

strains of Chopin
from the house next door
those late nights
when my aunt played piano
in the cold parlor

after midnight
the sound of peepers
in the darkness
remember the songs we sang
to scare away our fears?

it's mine now
Mother's old change purse
embroidered with beads—
snap of the clasp
as it opens and shuts

once-treasured keepsakes
now just shells and stones
collecting dust
my granddaughter wants them
to remember me by

turning thirteen
my granddaughter says
that she detests pink—
this unexpected sadness
of cherry blossom rain

in her cedar box
my baby hair clippings
and umbilical cord
what good will they do me now
forever untethered

CLEANING OUT THE ATTIC

under the eaves
my sister-in-law discovers
her wedding veil
  how gently she places it
    on top of her chemo hair

wedding presents
that were never opened—
two woolen blankets
still in their plastic wrappings
go to the grandchildren

a crochet champion—
my grandmother saved
all her gold ribbons
in a box labeled
with my sister's name

manila envelope
chocked full of photographs
of my youngest sister—
from honor student to model
to alcoholic recluse

from Mother's bookcase
a 1903 edition
of *Aesop's Fables*
I open the yellowed pages
and inhale my childhood

ALL THE DAY'S COLORS

the spring air
smells of rotting logs
wet and fecund
like beginnings and endings
with nothing in between

how will I return—
as a prince, pauper, or frog?
a mosquito whines
in my ear and tells me
not to aim so high

JUNCOS

junco courtship—
males riffle their wings
and hop up and down
I can't remember when
you were so glad to see me

weeding the garden
to rid my mind of clutter
tsk-tsk, tsk-tsk
a dark-eyed junco
adds twigs to her nest

in Japan
it's a woman's name—
wearing my *yukata*
I fill the birdfeeder
and call out "June-ko"

those bold eyes
behind black-feathered hoods
once
I donned a burka
to disappear

granddaughter in love
with dogs and horses
prances and gallops
around the house
while I feed her dog

on the eve
of the Year of the Tiger
I dream about our dog
who we left behind
his eyes burning bright

yellow jacket sting
I relieve the pain
with frozen packets
of organic blueberries
and homemade margaritas

waning moon
milkweed seeds burst
from their pods
the luna moth taut
in the owl's beak

midsummer's night
we gather some twigs
and start a campfire
all the day's colors
in the rainbow trout

when two roads diverge
I always take
the one less traveled—
blame it on all that Kool-Aid
I drank as a child

MEMALOOSE HILLS

Mosier, Oregon

what sweet innocence
Blue-eyed Marys blooming
along the trail—
those unblinking eyes
of my childhood dolls

queen of the spring
yellow balsamroot—
when they bloom
it's time for rattlesnakes
to come out from their dens

ten hikers
all stop at once
to take photos—
ten views of Mt. Hood
while standing in poison oak

from Marsh Hill
we look down on
the Island of the Dead—
like wildflowers, the graves
all facing east

yellow swallowtails
flit around clusters
of lupine and larkspur
tonight all my dreams
will be in color

playing hide and seek
I was always afraid
I'd never be found
the welcome sound
of the dinner bell

end of summer
I lie in the hammock
in my white lace skirt
and watch the hibiscus
fold up its petals

writing retreat
I walk the labyrinth
for the last time
resisting the urge
to pull up weeds

feeling uneasy
in the dead quiet
of the night desert
I take comfort
in the howl of coyotes

Oregon autumn—
gray skies, drizzle
and drenched dog walkers
I bask beneath the glow
of my yellow umbrella

a perfect mosaic
of aspen leaves
fallen on the pond
   doing what I want to do
      a duck swims through them

after all these years
I still miss you—
the patter
of steady rain
on ripe persimmons

an autumn day
spent reading poems
aloud to myself—
in the darkening pond
a snowy egret

evening of snow
I awake at midnight
from a bad dream
a full moon is glowing
behind scattered clouds

frozen igloos
we made as children
the simplicity of
one door in
one door out

blown back and forth
to the rhythm of Mahler
bare tree branches—
my house is dark
and smells of onions

FOOTLOOSE AND FANCY-FREE

footloose and fancy-free
I was once like the turtle
as I traveled the world
carrying my home
on my back

in Sri Lanka
climbing the rocky trail
to World's End
we chant to scare off
the chuffing leopard

SUMMER SOLSTICE AT THE GRAND CANYON

just before dawn
tourists ride mules
into the canyon
I'd rather soar
on the wings of a condor

at 7,000 feet
why am I so breathless—
all those years trekking
with everything I needed
on my back

from an outcropping
like a Tibetan prayer flag
a white yucca
motionless
in one-hundred degree heat

watch out, fashionistas
for rabid squirrels—
they will bite your red,
blue, green, or orange toenails
thinking they're M&M's

yellow as honey
a rare Strawberry Moon
on the Summer Solstice
the pungent tang of sagebrush
still clings to my clothes

gentle Ariadne
gave Theseus a ball of thread
to find his way home
who will help me navigate
the labyrinth of my heart?

spring in Krakow—
sleeping in a four-poster bed
we wake up to
the clip-clop of horse carts
on wet cobblestones

refugees huddle
in makeshift shelters
stench of mold
and urine-soaked mattresses
seep into their dreams

solitary walk
through the jungle—
on the path before me
a boa constrictor
asleep in his shadow

Zen Mountain Monastery

Mt. Tremper, New York

Buddhist retreat
this clover, too
is lit by summer sun
I practice humility
kneeling in the shadows

after last night's heat
wind stirs the ancient trees
their verdant leaves
rising and falling
like my breath

two fawns in the woods
only one stays and listens
to my sweet nothings
if only you
had been the one to stay

buzzing around
my floral umbrella
an errant bee
once I thought bright colors
would make me happy

leaving
the *zafus* and chanting
and incense behind
my suitcase
feels too heavy

zafu: a round cushion used in Zen meditation

seven years
since I last saw autumn
in the Sentō Gosho
golden fans of gingko leaves
are still fluttering

a young girl
claps her hands
to call the koi—
the stone Buddha's palms
clasped in *gassho*

Sentō Gosho: Imperial Palace in Kyōto, formerly for
retired emperors
gassho: palms of the hands placed together in a
prayer or greeting

making her way
with her umbrella cane
an old woman
strolls through the garden
of renewed moss

at Saihō-ji Temple
sitting on Musō's
meditation rock
the same green moss
and raucous crows

Musō Soseki: Japanese Zen priest and garden
designer

TRADITIONAL POETRY FESTIVAL

Jonangu Shrine, Kyōto, Japan

framed by green leaves
three priests in white robes—
late afternoon sun
filters through the sleeves
of the *koto* players

tsuwabuki flowers
rising to the sun
leave shadows
on the royal curtains—
the stream runs softly

Lady Murasaki
dressed in silken robes
of green and red—
the old man next to me
smells of mildew

as the *sake* cup
floats downstream
poets write *waka*
on paper strips—
approaching autumn

Heian-era poems
chanted by priests
in light blue *hakama*—
the distant hills, a brocade
of Nishiki weaving

koto: thirteen-stringed Japanese zither
tsuwabuki: daisy-like flower that grows by streams
waka: classical Japanese poem written in five lines
hakama: skirt-like pants worn by priests, martial artists,
and theater performers

sacred Mt. Fuji
home of the Immortals
hidden in clouds—
like Issa's snail
I climb it slowly, slowly

first dream of the year
snow-capped Mt. Fuji
suddenly
this world of black and white
becomes a blush of sunrise

winter afternoon
rain splatters
off temple roof tiles
　　the steady flow of ink
　　　from the calligrapher's brush

　　　　　　　where is she buried
　　　　　　　the imperial nun I taught
　　　　　　　at Jakko-in
　　　　　　　the temple we once sat in
　　　　　　　now boarded up and cold

waking from a nap
sun through the *shōji*
warms my face
the sweet potato seller
chants from the street

plum blossoms
against a gray sky
a tinge of red
daubed on the cheeks
of the aging courtesan

shōji: a sliding wooden door comprised of an open
lattice covered with a single layer of translucent
paper

Heian court ladies
dragged layers of kimonos
down dark corridors
those unfulfilled dreams I carry
into the new year

ACKNOWLEDGMENTS

Heartfelt thanks to Michael Dylan Welch for providing an introduction and for offering valuable comments and suggestions in earlier versions. Much appreciation to Patricia Donegan, Clemens Starck, and Patrick Donnelly for taking time to read the manuscript and contributing a blurb. As always, special thanks to John Hall for his steadfast support, for offering the author's photograph, and for proofreading the manuscript in its final stage. Lastly, I am grateful to have such a professional, aesthetic, and hard-working publisher. Thank you, Susan Gardner, for your guidance in bringing this book into the world.

Awards

cradled in my palm: First Prize, British Haiku Society
        International Tanka Contest, 2019
deadheading: Commended Winner, Second Kokato
        Contest, 2008
second grade: *The Skylark's Nest* Prompt Winner,
        Winter, 2016
childhood Halloweens: Global Haiku Contest, Finalist,
        2015
after the rain: Certificate of Merit conferred by
        Honmishoten Corporation for the 8th
        International Tanka Festival Contest, 2017
at Trader Vic's: Honorable Mention, World Tanka
        Competition, 2017
in my dream: Second Prize, The San Francisco
        International Competition for Haiku, Senryu,
        and Tanka, 2019
kaleidoscope night: Featured in the video journal,
        Frameless Sky: Fusion of Japanese Poetry and
        Music, 2017
plum blossoms: Featured in the video journal,
        Frameless Sky: Fusion of Japanese Poetry
        and Music, 2016
playing hide and seek: Haiku Poets of Northern
        California, Tanka Contest Award, 2012
refugees huddle: *tanka 2020, poems from today's
        world*, Red Moon Press, 2020
sacred Mt. Fuji: Fujisan Taisho International Tanka
        Festival, Honorable Mention, 2017
first dream of the year: Fujisan Taisho International
        Tanka Festival, Honorable Mention, 2018

Journals and Anthologies

Individual tanka appeared in:

Gusts
Ribbons (Tanka Society of America)
Moonbathing
Eucalypt (Australia)
Simply Haiku
A Hundred Gourds (Australia)
Skylark (England)
Bright Stars Anthology
Tanka Society of America Anthology
Ash Moon Anthology
Atlas Poetica
The Helping Hand Anthology

Tanka series appeared in:

Cleaning Out the Attic: *Ribbons*, Winter 2017
Juncos: *Ribbons*, Spring 2014
Memaloose Hills: *Ribbons*, Fall 2016
Obon at the Japanese Garden: *Ribbons*, Spring 2013
Snapshots, Juncos: *Ribbons*, Spring 2014
Sound of Peepers: *Ribbons*, Winter 2015
Taking a Turn: *Red Lights*, 2014
Traditional Poetry Festival: *Ribbons*, Fall 2018
Zen Mountain Monastery: *Ribbons*, Winter 2018